#RESTAURANTLIFE

*Lessons That Taught Me How to Become a
Successful Entrepreneur*

"If anything is good to pound humility into you permanently, it's the restaurant business."

– Anthony Bourdain

#RESTAURANTLIFE

*Lessons That Taught Me How to Become a
Successful Entrepreneur*

Tina Marie Wilken

PROFIT PROJECT
MONEY MINDSET MISSION

#RESTAURANTLIFE

Lessons That Taught Me How to Become a Successful Entrepreneur

Independently published by The Profit Project LLC. Profit Project and logos thereof are trademarks of The Profit Project LLC.
www.profitproject.co

First Edition | September 2019
ISBN 9781687388643 Paperback

In an effort to support local communities, raise awareness, and funds, Tina Marie Wilken and The Profit Project LLC donates a percentage of all book sales for the life of the book to the Women's Business Center at the YWCA Southern Arizona.

To Learn More, visit:
https://ywcatucson.org

DEDICATION

To my mother and father, who taught me resourcefulness, entrepreneurship, and to always be of service because that's how you show you care.

To my husband, who has always seen my true worth even when I couldn't. Who has never let me quit on myself and makes a mean taco. Thank you for supporting my bazillion million-dollar ideas.

To my HighWire Lounge family. Thank you for letting me go after my dreams, supporting me, and being all around the best. I will never see Chamoy and Pop Rocks the same.

Contents

ACKNOWLEDGEMENTS

First and foremost, I want to thank my many bosses and mentors throughout my career. I have learned so much about the industry, business, and life from each and every one of you.

To Tim Tracy who taught me the importance of feeling out people and intentions when interviewing new talent. Skills you can train but whether they'll fit in with the company culture or values, you can't. Thank you for the many life advice you've given me through a tough time. I will always take with when buying a home, scope it out around 8-10 pm at night. You really get to know the neighborhood at that time of day. Also, it's a marathon, not a race.

To Aaron Priestley who taught me that creating a fun, safe environment can make a team more productive. I was such a hard ass, still am, but I'm better at meeting the staff where they're at and supporting them. Team morale is bigger than bureaucracy and rules. People make the company, so treat them well. Let's Make it Happen.

There have been many individuals, co-workers, and regulars who have touched me, taught me, supported me, and become my family. To my Outback crew, I see you growing your beautiful families and even though we've drifted apart, you're all always in my thoughts. Thank you. You have all helped me grow into the person that I am now. I only hope to continue to grow to become a better person and boss.

To my Fox & Hound family, here's to some of the wildest times I have ever had in my life and some of the most cherished friendships I'll have for the rest of my life. Fox is where I met my husband, Tyler, and I'll be forever grateful for that.

To the Sully's crew, although a short time, it was sweet. I miss those office chats that had nothing to do with business but we could all still get our work done. Who said chefs, event planners, and admins can't get along?

Last but not least, a huge thank you to Nick and John of HighWire Lounge. You've taught me to be a better bartender and a lot about the bar industry. You have become part of my family. You will never know how much I am grateful to have met you both.

A huge thank you to Chef Gary Hickey and the Flores Family for supporting me in this endeavor. Thank you for allowing me to shoot my cover at your amazing Charro Vida location and allowing me to host my book launch party at the incredible Charro Del Rey.

It what was an unlikely career for me has turned out to be the best education on life and business anyone could ask for. My career has seen my worst ups and best downs. I will be forever grateful for the restaurant/bar industry for making me the person that I am today and for the amazing people in my life.

PREFACE

I've spent my whole working career in the restaurant/bar industry. 17 years. I never thought I'd stay in this industry but that's what it does. It lures and seduces you into its excitement, drama, stress, and pure passion for the art of food and cocktails. I started as a hostess. Like many college students, I needed a job that paid fairly well and had a flexible schedule, because I had big dreams after college.

Life took an unexpected turn, like it does for so many, and what became a job out of convenience became my lifeline. This book is both a love letter and thank you to my years in the industry and I'm not done with it yet. I moved my ambitious self all the way into management. Yet, I never aspired to be a general manager. There was something always tugging at me that I was meant for more.

I've worked at mom and pop places, corporate restaurants, craft mixology bars, and even opened a Panera store. I've done everything but run the back of the house but now I own my own catering company.

This world has been my MBA in business, truly. The experiences I've been through, lessons I learned, and skills acquired have forever shaped me to be a better boss, CEO, and leader.

I was inspired to write this book because as I looked back at my career, I realized that the lessons I learned were transferable to running my online business, my catering company, and now I hope to share it to help so many others.

This book is valuable because it will not only teach you practical business practices but hopefully inspire you to look at your own career and see what skills you've cultivated to help you in your journey into entrepreneurship. Regardless, of what your background is and where you want to go, our experiences help shape us to be leaders today.

This book was intentionally broken down into the different facets of a business but speaks directly to the owner or CEO... *you*. Through my experiences and lessons, you'll see areas that you'll want to improve or implement or know what you're doing well at.

This book was written for the small business owner, freelancer, solopreneur, dreamer, and entrepreneur in mind. If there is anything I've learned through my entrepreneurial journey, is that relearning the basics never hurts, and continuous growth is always a good sign of sustainability, for the individual and business.

So, thank you for spending your time with this book. Let's dive in.

CHAPTER 1

Branding

Branding had to be one of the biggest lessons I learned, more importantly, personal branding. I was a quiet, shy introvert wanting to become a server (*that's where the real money was*). My boss, to say the least was...*hesitant*, and rightfully so. I hate small talk and the idea of having to do so was frightening. Why couldn't I just do my job → take your order, bring your food, bring your check, you pay and we all be on our merry way. I love efficiency and just wanted to do what I do best. My work.

The image I put out was not of a person who could handle the sales and relationship building side of serving. So, what's a quiet, shy girl to do? I mean, bills had to get paid. I had to really change the self-image I was putting out there and most importantly, I had to grow.

I quickly had to learn who I was, what I had to offer, and how to build a rapport with guests. I love a challenge, so I made it a game. Every shift, every table, I tried different ways to connect with my guests. How do I get them to enjoy the experience and be efficient as well? How do I enjoy this experience and still hit every corporate mark?

It took me about six months to understand people go out to eat for the experience just as much as the food. It wasn't about the meal being made by someone else, it was about escaping school stress, work stress, or having a special night out with family and friends.

Branding is more than themes, colors, and logos. Although it's important, it's truly about your company's personality, what they stand for, and what they offer. People connect with people and feelings, as much as they say they make decisions based on logic. It's really all about the connections and relatability. So, whoever you work with, such as vendors, partners, influencers, and those on your team are a reflection of your brand as well.

Whether you're creating a personal brand or a company brand, you need to define who you are, how you want the world to perceive you, and how you're going to communicate to create a connection.

WHO ARE YOU?

Whenever we describe businesses to other people, we often use adjectives like we would about a person. "*Oh, Blue Willow? I love that place! It's clean, friendly, and fast.*" So, start thinking about your business as a person. What values and beliefs do you hold?

What's your purpose? Who are you and how do you connect with people?

Our personalities define how we act, interact with people, dress, and communicate. Your business is no different. Does your brand match your ideal clients? Are you putting out the right vibes to attract the right customers?

How I carried myself and spoke to guests when I worked at the sports bar, fine dining restaurant, and ultra-lounge bar were all different. I could be more casual and talk like one of the guys at the sports bar. At the fine dining restaurant, I was more poised and professional. At the ultra-lounge bar, I would talk as an expert on drinks, spirits, and new things going on in the bar industry because it was a craft cocktail bar, known for creations you couldn't get anywhere else.

When I created my coaching company, I forgot about how much I needed to define brand in this way. I started out thinking the same as everyone else. Get a logo, pick some colors, and let's get going. The more I studied branding, remembered my career, I started to understand what I really needed to do. What did I want my brand to be remembered for?

DESIGN TO IMPRESS

Now, I know I mentioned branding is more than themes, colors, and logos. It's all in how you make people feel. However, there is something to say about the look and feel of your company should match your company's or your (for personal branding) personality.

Your logo should be reflective of your style, what you do, and who you are. Your colors, font, and style should match the vibe you want to give people when they interact with your brand. That's why is critical to know who you are and how you want to communicate.

So, when creating your brand identity and style, think about:

- Color psychology and color theory
- What fonts you'll use
- What's your style? Is it colorful, clean, minimal, modern, vintage, etc.

Consistency is key here. Using comic sans (I know no one would) for a luxury brand doesn't match. Using dark colors for a brand that reaches kids doesn't work either.

MESSAGING

Outback Steakhouse® lived and breathed their theme and values. From the moment of orientation, through training, and all the way to the quality of food & service, they lived and breathed their brand. It may have been cheesy at times, but it created an air of fun and it left nothing to interpretation.

At the time I worked there, everyone who came to Outback knew they were getting quality, housemade dishes and sauces. Even their 12 different salad dressings were made from scratch. A staff in bright colored shirts and flair was a sight to behold. I hated those shirts and pins but you would not believe how many people asked about the different pins we wore. I still think they're collector's items.

From the people you work with, to the people who work for you and your customers, EVERYONE who comes in contact with your brand needs to know where you stand, your values, and what you do best. This is so incredibly important to make clear and help your brand stand-out.

The people who work with you and for you are also a living representation of your brand, so be sure to vet them and make sure they align well with your brand and you. This includes influencers or celebrity endorsers.

CONSISTENCY

If your brand messaging is clear and specific, then consistency shouldn't be an issue. The devil is in the details, they say, and it's true. Don't stray away in the hopes of attracting a new demographic or increasing sales, you'll only hurt your brand in the long run. You wouldn't expect to get chips & salsa at Olive Garden, would you? It'd be a bit confusing, right? So, know your vision and mission statement and make sure all your products and services match.

It is one thing for your brand to grow with the times and as your target market has grown into something different organically. However, don't let fear dictate your decisions. Don't worry about what your competitors is doing well. Keep doing you, create loyal fans and live and breathe your brand.

HAVE A SIGNATURE ITEM

I cannot tell you how many people came in for the signature appetizer, the Bloomin' Onion®. Almost everyone who came through the doors bought it, asked about it, or came because they heard about it. That my friend is what you want, BRAND RECOGNITION.

You need a signature item that brings in new clients, still have complimentary products, but have that main product or service you are known for. If you are starting out, focus on marketing just this product/service. Gain testimonials, loyal fans and then you can build other products to compliment it and build on it.

ADAPTABILITY

Although, long gone are the days of bright colored shirts and flair at Outback. They have evolved with the current tastes and culture, but still kept their original brand values and personality in tack. There menu still boasts colorful themed names, and the décor still gives a sense of Australian but modernized to fit the current market tastes.

We live in a fast-growing world economy. Regardless if your small business is targeted to a local community or you provide services worldwide, the immediate access of the internet has had an influence on culture, society, and market tastes, so you need to pay attention.

This doesn't mean you change your whole brand every time your ideal client changes their needs and wants. Learn how to pivot your brand to always be relevant in current times while still staying true to your values, mission, and overall authenticity.

CHAPTER 2

Marketing

Marketing and sales go beyond business. We have to sell ourselves all the time, to our bosses, spouses, friends, etc. a part of persuading others is building a *"Know, Like, and Trust"* factor. They need to know you well, like you enough to buy from you, and trust you'll take care of them. Establishing this factor and how you deliver your promises, is imperative to executing clear marketing strategies. I learned creating relationships created repeat customers, not just for the restaurant but for me.

KNOW YOUR AUDIENCE

If you don't know who you're selling to then you won't make sales. You can try to appeal to everyone but the more general you are, the more likely you won't connect with anyone. This makes marketing harder and well...your brand forgettable.

Don't get me wrong, you don't have to be so niche where you're literally a specialty (unless you are) but you need to be really focused on who you serve, so you can always be of value.

Let's think about it in my career. Some examples below are corporate well-known restaurants that I've worked at:

> *Outback Steakhouse®: It's a casual dining restaurant. Targeting lower to middle income guests. Family friendly. Get great food for reasonable prices, with a sit-down relaxing environment but quick service.*

> *Fox & Hound Bar & Grill: A sports bar with several rooms to accommodate several sporting events. For sports enthusiasts and fans to watch their favorite team with their friends and family. Full menu of beers, full-service bar and a menu to satisfy any appetite.*

> *Sullivan's Steakhouse: A fine dining steakhouse. Guests looking to celebrate special occasions or want a nice meal and aren't in a rush. The menu is pricier, so guests are usually of the kind with more disposable income to spend.*

> *Panera Bread: A fast casual concept. Fresh baked bread and pastries. Targeting the breakfast crowd and quick lunches but with a sit-down feel.*

These are all established and successful restaurants that serve food and drinks but each one serves a specific type of clientele.

So, when you're thinking about your branding, who are you serving?

Understanding who you're serving helps formulate your brand, marketing plan, products/services, and your company vision. Below are a few questions you should ask yourself when you're figuring out who you serve.

1. Demographics: (What's their age, gender, marital status, location, occupation, job title, annual income, ethnicity, level of education, kids, own or rent, etc.?)
2. Their challenges and pain points. (What are they struggling with?)
3. Dreams & personal values (Do they want financial freedom, security, or happiness? A fun time versus an educational time? Do they value family, integrity, transparency, etc.?)
4. Personality & Interests (Are they funny or serious? What shows do they watch or watch tv at all, magazines/blogs they read, radio/podcasts they listen to, music, role models, large events they attend, hobbies, etc.? Where do they hang out?)

DEMOGRAPHICS

Some of these items may seem trivial but they paint a picture of the type of client/customer you're working with. Knowing how much they make a year; you can gauge what their lifestyle is like. Knowing what job they have and position, you can gauge, "How much time do they have?" These demographics begin to shape a broad picture of your clientele and will help in answering some of those questions.

CHALLENGES & PAIN POINTS

Find out what challenges and pain points your ideal client has in regards to the product or service you provide. Let's take a look at the corporate restaurants I listed previously and see what their clientele may be looking for.

Outback Steakhouse:
- College students, young professionals, and young families with not a lot of extra time to cook.
- Not a lot of extra disposable income, so looking for value
- Wants delicious food that's not from a drive thru all the time but still affordable.

Fox & Hound Bar & Grill:
- Needing a place where a group can get together and watch their favorite team games with a good food selection and drink specials.
- A place with good food, great beer selection and be able to catch up and watch multiple sports games versus just one at home.
- Looking for a place that has activities (like darts, pool, etc.) versus just sitting down at a bar.

Sullivan's Steakhouse
- Looking for an elevated dining experience.
- Great wine selection and knowledge.
- High quality ingredients.
- Great atmosphere for celebrating special occasions.

Panera Bread

- Families, millennials, baby boomers.
- Generally busy and middle income to high earners who eat out more often and want the experience of a restaurant but the quick pace of service as a fast food restaurant.
- Are health conscious eaters looking for reasonably priced, tasty, and quick service for breakfast and lunch options.

Just like the different restaurants listed above, you may be one in the sea of business coaches, photographers, accountants, social media marketer, etc., but knowing who your client base is and what they're struggling with helps you stand out from the crowd.

DREAMS & PERSONAL VALUES

You may not think you need to understand your client's life dreams and personal values, but it will help you delve into the psychology of what drives them to buy.

There was a guy who weighed over 400 pounds and would eat about 10,000 calories a day. He struggled fitting into doorways, vehicles, and dealt with health and sleep issues caused by his excessive weight. One day he fell asleep at the wheel and drove his car into a ditch. When he woke up from the nightmare, he decided he needed to make a drastic change.

A year later he lost 245 pounds by combining exercise and eating sandwiches from... Subway. Yes, you remember Jared, right? Jared's dream of losing weight and getting healthy made the company go from fast food chain to global lifestyle brand. Subway was no longer just another place to grab sub sandwiches with fresh ingredients, it was a brand that could boast about eating fresh AND healthy, in the ocean of greasy, unhealthy fast food choices.

So, ask yourself, what are the most important things in the world to your client? What do they value most? Is it integrity, family, good health, work life balance, etc.? Then ask yourself, "How does this pertain to the products/services I provide?" It doesn't have be a complete life altering transformation you provide, maybe it's an escape from life's stress.

PERSONALITY & INTERESTS

What kind of person is your ideal client? Now that we have a little idea of demographics, challenges, and personal values, we can drill down on the type of person they are. What are they reading, watching, and listening to? Do they hang out online? Are they on social media, and forum websites like Reddit or Quora?

PROMOTION

In the days before social media marketing, businesses had to get creative with promotions and advertising, especially restaurants. There hasn't been one restaurant I've worked at that didn't give out a free appetizer or dessert cards to draw people into the restaurant. I mean who doesn't like free food? This was just one promotional activity of three that really stood out to me, which I apply today.

FREEBIES AND DISCOUNTS

Now, giving out free stuff isn't something new but can be tough for many small and new businesses to swing. So how can you apply this to your business? The free appetizer or dessert cards were given to potential guests and even current ones already dining in. The idea behind it, is to give them a reason to come in and for new people, a reason to try something.

If you got a free appetizer or dessert, would you really only get that? Most likely, you'll get a couple of drinks for happy hour or sit down for a meal. Yes, there might be some people who would take advantage of it and not get anything else, but it still accomplished them trying the product. They may share it with someone else who comes with them or rave about it to others. This is all a win for you.

Here are some examples based on the type of business you may be in:

> *E-commerce/Retail: free sample products with purchase, one regular sized product free (they pay for shipping or come into the store), % discount for email exchange or $$, free samples in exchange for reviews)*

> *Services: free consultations, free low-level services that might lead to selling bigger services (i.e. free massage from a chiropractor, free cleanings from a dentist,*

tastings for a caterer, free custom invitations for an event planner.)

For any business (online/offline): free How-to Guides, checklists, video trainings, webinars in exchange for their emails. The items listed here help establish you as an expert in your field and/or provide value.

OUTREACH & NETWORKING

Creating connections with the community and doing free events was a staple for a couple of my bosses. At different points in my career, I worked events sponsored by the restaurant to our local college athletic programs, local nonprofits, and local events. It was a great way for the brand to live its mission and values and also promote brand and product recognition in the local community.

VENDOR PARTNERSHIPS AND NETWORK

Finding partners who are complimentary to your industry and creating relationships is advantageous. The bars I worked at would work closely with our liquor representatives to create promotional events or support each other's events. This drove guests through our doors and therefore more sales for us and we'd promote their products so therefore more sales and brand recognition for them.

Don't discount creating relationships and partnering with someone you might deem the competition. Working at a downtown bar, we'd be part of bar crawls and after parties for local events. By cross promoting all the bars, we increase the attendance to all our establishments.

Maybe you're a massage therapist that mainly works with pre-natal moms and you know of another massage therapist that works strictly with the elderly or athletes. You all can give each other referrals. Or whatever you do, you might do the same thing and can't take on clients at this. You have someone you can refer your clients to (vice versa) and that's added value of taking care of them even though you're not the one providing the product/service.

CUSTOMER LOYALTY

It is far more affordable for a business to retain a customer than to acquire one. It can cost up to five times more to get a new customer versus keeping one. † It is also more likely that a current customer will buy again from you and refer you. So, why do we spend so much money on getting new customers?

AN AMAZING CUSTOMER EXPERIENCE
There are several small and low-cost ways to keep customers loyal! Making the whole buying experience smooth, fun, and memorable is the first key to building a lasting relationship with customers. Wowed customers return. I talk more about creating an overall amazing customer experience in chapter 5.

Keep the customers engaged with your brand. Whether it is inviting them back to try items coming out, create fun and engaging posts on social media, or email them updates from your newsletter, keeping your brand top of mind is critical.

REWARDS PROGRAMS

Several restaurants I worked at had a rewards program. Rewards programs are a great way to keep your customers loyal to your brand. They are specifically designed to keep people coming back to shop with you. They are generally free to sign up, you receive bonus points for signing up, and usually have a specific point structure per dollars spent to rack up discounts or dollars to spend towards future purchases.

At Fox & Hound, when I worked there, you'd get 25 points just for signing up, the more you spent in your lifetime, you'd progress up a value ladder. The more money a customer spends, they move up the value ladder to receive bigger and better perks. This encourages the customer to spend more with you and possibly exclusively with you. (*See example on the next page.*)

There are different ways to create a rewards program that works for you. Rewards programs work best for actual products (physical or digital) versus services. You can create a point system like the one above, create a monthly VIP membership where customers get exclusive items not available to the general public, or combine different loyalty program strategies to increase value.

As I build up my online academy, any clients can purchase each class separately, therefore only purchase what they need or want. Or they can pay for the monthly membership and get access to all my classes for the lifetime of their membership and monthly coaching in a private group.

Get creative regardless of what you do. Are you a service provider? Have a special VIP email list or Facebook community that gets exclusive trainings, updates, and bonuses. They are the first to know about new product or service offerings and discounts or specials.

See Example of a tier rewards program from Sephora:

2019 Beauty Insider Benefits

		INSIDER	VIB	ROUGE
(P)	Points per $1 ▶	1 point	1.25 points	1.5 points
	Birthday gift ▶	2 choices	4 choices	4 choices
	Seasonal savings ▶	$	$ $	$ $ $
	Tier celebration gift ▶		1 choices	1 choices
	Free standard shipping ▶			●
	Early access to products ▶			●
	Exclusive events ▶			●
	Rewards Bazaar* ▶	●	●	●
NEW!	$100 Rouge Reward			●

https://sleeknote.com/blog/customer-loyalty-programs

CHAPTER 3

Products/Services

I struggled with product and service creation for a long time! Full transparency, I struggled hard my first 3 years on getting into a flow of how I wanted to serve and how to serve. I thought it was simple. I have massive experience, went to school, and I was still actively working in the industry to teach other people, so obviously I can call myself a coach and work by the hour.

Although, I saw some success, it wasn't at the level I had expected in the beginning. It wasn't until I got really clear on who I was, what I wanted my brand to be, and who I wanted to serve, is when things fell into place.

The first two chapters should give you a clear idea of who you are as a brand and who you serve. Armed with this knowledge, creating products/services should be much easier. I look back at when I got to contribute to menus with item ideas, it was the same as it would be for my own business.

We're going to talk about the customer mapping, passive and active income, and the business of getting paid.

THE CUSTOMER JOURNEY

The customer journey mapping is usually described in terms of the customer's journey with you during the buying cycle. How you attract them, how'll they purchase, what happens after purchasing, etc. I'm using the term "customer journey" in terms of where they are at personally and the likelihood, they'll buy a specific product/service.

For example, when we would be brainstorming and creating cocktails for HighWire Lounge (a craft mixology bar in downtown Tucson), we would map out which types of cocktails we needed to serve based on our brand and our clientele. We would have our premium signature cocktails that displayed the creativity of molecular mixology, cocktails that used local distilleries, lighter cocktails that are good for any occasion, and a few cocktails in between.

We'd make sure we had a fine balance of representing different liquors. We didn't want to be a list of only bourbon cocktails or vodka cocktails. On the same side, we didn't want to have all sugary sweet drinks or liquor heavy drinks. By keeping that balance, we'd have a menu that would appeal to both men and women, gin and whiskey drinkers alike.

When you're brainstorming on what products/services to provide, sit down and map out who your ideal client is, how you serve, keep your brand values in mind, and ask yourself these questions:

1. How does my ideal client want to use my product/service?
2. Is my industry seasonal?
3. Do I have a good balance of products/services that can meet my customer's needs at any stage?
4. What value does the product/service bring?

PASSIVE & ACTIVE INCOME

When I first started my coaching business, I only offered 1:1 coaching by the hour. Although I had a few clients, it was stressful and became a job to me. When you are swapping time for money, it is still just like employment.

Restaurants I worked at didn't have anything in place to create passive income, but they did diversify their offerings. This doesn't mean they created new items, but rather expanded on some of their existing favorites. For example, when I worked at Outback Steakhouse®, they made their dressings from scratch. The ranch dressing was so good; we'd often get customers calling in just to buy the ranch dressing! There are several restaurants out there who have a product line you can find in grocery stores and some even have retail products like branded clothing and accessories.

Some restaurants have found different ways to serve. For example, booking private events, catering, and to go ordering. These seem pretty standard these days but it took someone to sit down and see how else they could serve their customers.

You can create offerings in both products and services regardless of what you do and bring value. Don't believe me? Let's take the example of a realtor. Some passive income ideas for a realtor are to have their own rental property or AirBnB type property, write a book (*yes, a book! Are you an expert in Antebellum architecture or Midcentury design? Talk about it. Do you specialize in finding homes for military personnel? Write about it. An expert in getting low income, low or no credit first time buyers a good home. Write that book.*), teach workshops or create e-courses based on your niche expertise.

There are plenty of opportunities to bring in money both passively and actively regardless of what you do. You just have to have the mindset to create and imagine it!

GET PAID

I saw your eyes get big. This is everyone's favorite subject. In this section, I'm not going to teach you pricing strategies and how to price for profit. That is a whole other book in itself and future digital course in my online academy. What I will talk about is making it easy for your customers to pay you and get great service.

Two things I've learned from the restaurant/bar industry when it comes to taking payments:

1.) Give them several options to pay. You eliminate any reason why they can't purchase.
2.) Make it as quick and easy as possible.

It's common knowledge that when you go to a restaurant, the server will drop off your check, run your card and bring it back to you, so you never have to leave the table. Nowadays, fast casual restaurants are making the process faster, where you order and pay up front and the food is brought to you. When you're done, you can leave.

Ways you can make the purchasing process faster and easier:

- Allow all types of payments to be used
- Offer to come to them
- Pay online
- Set up automatic payments for recurring payments

The faster you get paid, the better your cash flow is.

CHAPTER 4

Sales

Remember in chapter one when I said I was a shy, quiet girl wanting to be a server? Well, I will never forget the day I asked my boss to become a server, I had just turned 19 and it was the minimum age in our state where you could serve alcohol.

I saw the look in my boss's eyes and heard the *hesitation* in his voice. It didn't deter me. It took me a couple of weeks (*in reality probably month*s) to convince him to give me a try. Like any 19-year-old college kid at the time, I was motivated by money to pay the bills and get through school. So, between that motivation and the confidence that I'd excel, I set out to learn everything I could.

It was a rude awakening to learn, although I was an employee of a corporation, as a server, I was running my own business that just happened to supply me with warm to hot leads. It would be up to me to create amazing experiences where the guests could tip me more and come back and ask for me. Or if anything, come back to keep the restaurant open another day, another shift.

Sales is the life force of any business. You MUST GET COMFORTABLE with sales if you want to grow your business! These are the crucial lessons I learned about sales: sales strategy, creating customer loyalty, and the sales pipeline.

SALES STRATEGY

I don't blame my boss for his hesitation because of my quiet nature. I was going to suck at sales...and *I did.* I hated small talk because of the type of personality I had, it has no substance to me. To my frustration, I made money but not nearly as much as some of my more outgoing co-workers.

I didn't make it to the top of the sales competitions (which irked me, because I am one of the most competitive people in the world). To be a better salesperson, I decided to watch and ask those who were on top and use my introvert superpowers: the power of observation and reading people.

In restaurants, they always want you to offer an appetizer, add a salad or soup, alcoholic beverage, whatever entrée feature of the day, and dessert. There is a higher profit margin in drinks, so the suggestion there is obvious. If you can get a table to get all four courses, you've brought up your check average, which in turn adds more sales and possibly higher tips for the server.

The five things that make great sales AND customer experience:

1. Reading your clientele
2. Benefits vs Features
3. Know Your Products & Company inside and out
4. Upselling vs Cross selling
5. Always ask

READING YOUR CLIENTELE

How I would approach a group of college guys, family, or couple is completely different. The strategy was always the same but what products I'd suggest would be tailored to the table. I always made the signature item as a recommendation and then an appetizer that would fit the table. As I mentioned in chapter 3, your signature product/service should appeal to your ideal clientele, regardless of demographics.

Example:

- For large groups, college guys, and families → I'd suggest larger appetizers.
- For smaller families or medium sized groups → I'd suggest either a couple of different smaller appetizers for variety or a medium sized appetizer that feeds 2–4 people
- For couples, I'd suggest smaller appetizers that have 2–4 bites

By tailoring your suggestions to their needs/wants, you increase the opportunity of a yes. How does this translate to your business? In the last chapter, you should have fleshed out products and services that are wide ranging and can meet the customer's needs at any point in their journey.

BENEFITS VS. FEATURES

All too common people fail at sales and marketing because they focus on highlighting the features of a product/service versus the *benefits*. All people really want to know is, "What's in it for me?"

How you differentiate yourselves from the competition lies in the benefits of your products/services. Think in terms of results. What do they get out of it? When I worked at the steakhouses, I'd often get asked which size steak should they get or which steak should they get. After asking them a few questions, like what do they prefer, how do they like their steak temp to be and how hungry were they?

For example, let's say someone wants a tender cut of meat. I'd recommend the filet if they wanted the most tender cut of beef but I'd recommend the ribeye if they wanted something more flavorful. The marbling (streaks of fat throughout the cut) in the ribeye is a feature but the benefit is the flavor and tenderness that it provides.

Get familiar with the benefits of your products/services. Maybe you produce one of kind items, have fast service, luxury concierge at an affordable price, help people save money or time. Whatever it is, highlight those versus what the facts are.

Marbling		The	Adds tenderness and flavor
Bone-In or Boneless		Ribeye	Bone-In adds to the already bold flavoring
Versatile			Can be complimented with any sauce or none at all, as it's flavor stands all on its own.

KNOW YOUR OFFERINGS & COMPANY INSIDE OUT

It didn't matter which company I worked for, we would train, study, and be quizzed on new menu items. Our managers knew if we were equipped with the knowledge of what the products were and what they do, they would be easier to sell.

Product knowledge arms you with the confidence in selling. No one wants to be that sleezy salesman. When you know you have the product/service to solve someone's problems, it's alleviates any feelings of being pushy or sleezy. At the end of the day, if they say no to your suggestion, then it only means "not for me" or "not right now".

In depth product knowledge AND a large understanding of your company culture helps you weed out anyone who may not connect with you also. A big myth amongst business owners is, they need to appeal to everyone and they can't say no to a customer because they may miss out on a sale.

> *"Sales isn't about pushing a product on someone who may or may not need it, because you have numbers to make. It's about targeting the right people with the right solutions, so you can provide it better than anyone else."*

Sales isn't about pushing a product on someone who may or may not need it, because you have numbers to make. It's about targeting the right people with the right solutions, so you can provide it better than anyone else. There is no better way to provide value than knowing your products/services inside and out, who you serve, and how you serve.

UPSELLING VS. CROSS-SELLING

One of the biggest things I learned about selling is upselling and cross-selling. Upselling is providing a comparable but higher end product/service. Cross-selling is providing a product/service which compliments their current purchase.

Upselling Example:
Guest: "I'd like a vodka tonic."

Me: "Great! Would you like Belvedere, Grey Goose, Ketel One, Tito's, Smirnoff or our house selection?"

In this example, I started listing the higher end products and then trail down to our lower priced items. This a) educates them on what you carry b) Hopefully chooses a brand that they like and are familiar with before just settling on the most affordable item. Not everyone is going to pick premium but by upselling you gain the increased sales from customers who are willing to pay.

Cross-selling Example:
Guest: "I'd like the filet mignon medium rare please."
Me: "That's an excellent choice. Our medium rare is going to be a warm red center. Is that what you're looking for?
Guest: "Yes, that's perfect."
Me: "Great. Our filet mignon pairs very well with the bourbon cracked peppercorn sauce. We make it in house with Maker's Mark and fresh cracked peppercorns. Would you like to add that tonight?"

In this cross-selling example, I shared another product we offered which paired well with their current choice. I could have also suggested a specific wine that paired well with their meal. Cross-selling items are usually products/services that are about the same price to lower in price to the original item but compliments it very well.

Have you ever shopped for clothes online or on Amazon and they have those suggestions, "people who looked at this item, also looked at/bought this too."? That's cross selling.

ALWAYS ASK

I hated selling our specials of the day or promoting our company's rewards program. I felt it was intrusive and I was pushing the company's "agenda". I had a very negative outlook of the world back then. What I realized over time, by not asking, I made the decision for my guest. I made the assumption they wouldn't want it or would feel I was being pushy. By projecting that, when I did offer, I got rejected. People pick up your energy.

It was to my surprise, when I just challenged myself to ask everyone, I got more yeses than I ever thought I would. In fact, more times than not, when I applied this rule of asking everyone, I was always one of the top performers.

We often create these stories in our heads of outcomes or responses that may or may not happen. It's not our place to decide for other people. All we can do is offer them an option. It is up to them to decide, not you. Which leads me to the next section.

THE PIPELINE

On busy Friday and Saturday nights, while hostessing, my manager on duty would ask one of us to pass out samples. We would sample out the Bloomin' Onion®, cheese fries, and even desserts. The first time I saw this, I asked my manager why we did that? His answer was brilliant.

People who are hungry and have to wait an hour for dinner get cranky. If they're anything like me, hangry. By sampling out food, we killed three birds with one stone: create a hospitable waiting experience, entice the guest to order said item, keep people excited enough to endure the wait.

We would have some guests order an appetizer and ask for drinks while they waited for their table. What I learned was prospecting and lead generation in its simplest form. Now, granted the guests waiting were already people who wanted to eat at the restaurant but we don't know if they'll buy an appetizer or not, or leave because the wait is too long.

At its bare basic, a sales pipeline is about four to five steps and is the path of point A (Identifying potential customers) to point B (closing the sale).

1. Lead Generation
2. Lead Nuturing/Qualification
3. Proposal
4. Deal (Lost/Won)
5. Follow Up

The pipeline may be more intricate in bigger companies or the stages are called different things. For the sake of simplicity, this is what I use to breakdown my sales pipeline.

LEAD GENERATION

Lead generation is the process of generating interest in your products/services. There are cold leads (may or may not know of your products/services and may/may not be interested in buying) and there are warm leads (people who are interested in your products/services and are potential buyers).

There are several different lead generation strategies. From my story previously, we used sampling as a strategy. Giving something for free has long been a tried and true strategy for generating leads. It's a great way to sample some of your work and those who take your freebie, become warm leads. A warm lead is someone more likely to purchase from you, because you know they are interested in the information you are providing.

There are a few lead generating activities out there like content marketing, webinars, free trainings, e-books, industry reports, and networking. Regardless if you have an online or offline business, networking, social media, and content marketing are great ways to develop new leads.

LEAD NURTURING/QUALIFICATION

After handing out samples to our waiting guests, we would stop by pick up any trash and ask if they enjoyed the it. Whenever someone said it was good or they loved it, I would build a rapport and tell them what I loved about the product or what other people loved about it.

At this point I'm nurturing the idea of ordering said appetizer, either while they wait or with their server. Out of all my interactions, the ones that are most engaging with me or enthusiastic, were quality leads where the guests end up buying. Some may not have bought that night, but came back another time to buy. The lead nurturing phase is all about building trust and a relationship with your lead regardless if they're ready to buy right now or later. We're in it for the long game.

How do you nurture your leads? Email lists, social media or any media outlet they can subscribe to, phone calls, or direct mail. It takes on average about 6-8 touches with your lead before they buy. Therefore, consistent communication is key in keeping you top of mind.

This doesn't mean spam their inbox or call every day (unless your audience expects that). However, give your leads the opportunity to follow you in multiple places. Invite them to follow all your social media accounts, get them on your weekly newsletter, and have them subscribe to your podcast or YouTube channel.

THE PROPOSAL

This is where we do the big ask. At this point, you've built a solid *"Know, Like, and Trust"* factor, you know their major objections and have addressed them. They're familiar with who you are and what you can do. So, you present your product/service as the solution to their woes and offer them an opportunity to buy or work with you.

DEAL CLOSED (WIN/LOSE)

Now if the client buys or ends up working with you, that's a win! If they don't, that's okay. There are three things I learned when someone says no to the buy.

1. If they haven't provided a reason, I ask why.
2. Continue nurturing the relationship.
3. Analyze my sales process.

For the first step, I may or may not get new information but it'll help me with step 3. Know when you have an opportunity to convert to a sale at the time, maybe another time, or to let it go. You must be okay with letting it go. So many business owners are afraid of sales because we're afraid of rejection, but we have to understand that it's not personal.

We're either not presenting the solution in a way that's beneficial for them or understanding it may not be the right time. As a server, if someone said no and I still couldn't convert, then I'd move on with the dinner experience and still make them feel welcomed and taken care of. Giving them a great experience will make them want to come back.

Maybe today wasn't the right time but they'll make time (and money) for the next time. Just stay focused on providing value and move on to the next opportunity.

CHAPTER 5

The Customer Experience

I had the most intense on the job training than anywhere I've ever worked at Outback Steakhouse®. Maybe it felt that way because it set me up for every job I ever had, including non-restaurant jobs. At the young age of 19, I learned how to become a server. Outback prided itself on its quality ingredients but more importantly was its dedication to exceptional customer service.

Their standards of customer service were so strict but it taught me the value of letting people feel welcomed, seen and taken care of. The customer service experience from before they buy to after they buy should be smooth, amazing, and honestly over deliver. I'm a firm believer in under promising and over delivering, when it comes to service.

Now I'm not saying you need to compromise your values, resources, or stress yourself out for a customer. There is a difference between someone demanding things that are outside the scope of your abilities or resources. However, simply treating your customers like a valued part of your family does go a long, long way.

BE OUR GUEST

As you've seen throughout the book already, I call the customers in restaurants, guests. In the restaurant industry, it is standard to call customers guests because that's how we want to treat them, like guests in our home.

When you have guests in your home, you make sure your house is clean, greet them immediately, be respectful, and treat them like VIPs. Your customers/clients shouldn't be any different.

But Tina Marie, I get hundreds of orders a day for my products, how do I make them each feel special? I definitely get you don't have the bandwidth to reach every single customer that buys from you at that volume but there are many ways to automate thank you emails, choose five people to reach out and mail them a handwritten thank you card or give them a follow up call after a week of using your products.

Remembering personal details is always helpful in treating people like VIPs. Does your client have kids, anniversary coming up, favorite team or hobbies? These are great touch points.

Are you strictly online retail? On your order forms, ask their birthdays. When the day comes, send them a happy birthday email or better yet, a hand written thank you. Trust me it goes a long way.

ANTICIPATING WANTS/NEEDS

One of the biggest customer service strategies I learned was called "silent service". It's the idea of anticipating the needs of the customer and fulfilling them without the customer having to ask. If the customer was drinking water or ice tea, we were taught to automatically fill the glass when it was half full or bring a refill. The same went for the bread refills. When half the bread was gone, I'd just automatically bring another loaf.

Be mindful and observant of your customer's needs and wants. After a while, I could see patterns, body language, and general energy of the table to gauge whether to be present more, hang back, interact with the table or limit conversation, and eating or drinking habits.

Two real life examples of anticipating needs/wants to bring added value:

Event Planner:

I will never forget the night of our wedding. It had been a long day and go, go, go. As soon as we were introduced as husband and wife to everyone, we sat down. Within seconds of sitting down, the venue event planner and chef placed plates in front of us from the buffet. I've heard horror stories about brides and grooms not getting to eat because they were so busy. I'm so glad they took note of this from their experience and made sure we got to eat. This stood out to me more than anything else they did to make our day smooth and special and I am forever grateful for that.

Veterinarian:
Our dog, Arya had a serious infection in her paws. She was on antibiotics and steroids and testing showed she needed to be on a second antibiotic because she had two aggressive infections. Our vet mailed the prescription to our house so we didn't have to make a trip down there to get it. Also, knowing we had already spent a lot of money at a previous vet to find the problem and spent a lot on testing, she took the time to research the cheapest place to buy the antibiotic and even printed us a coupon too!

Those are prime examples of paying attention to your client's needs and going above and beyond to execute it without them ever asking, expecting, or even knowing they need it. What are some ways you can elevate the experience of buying from or working with you?

WELCOME WAGON

A good bartender will greet you as soon as you walk in the door no matter how busy they are with another guest. It may seem small and most of time when we walk in, we hardly notice it or seem to think it is special. Have you ever walked in a restaurant and not be greeted by someone who works there? You definitely notice then!

For all my one on one clients, I send them a welcome package with gifts and a handwritten thank you card. All my one on one clients have different goals they want to work through. During the breakthrough session, we flesh out what they want to improve in the next six months. I make sure to send them items that pertain to their goals, self-care and empowering gifts.

I always send an immediate thank you email to everyone who works with me or purchases from my site, whether they are joining a course or buying a coffee cup, they get an immediate acknowledgement and gratitude.

You don't always have to give gifts to welcome them. Just acknowledging people goes a long way. When someone tags you on social media, makes a comment on your post, or in any way engages with your brand, respond back immediately!

The biggest thing about business building and continued growth, is cultivating and nurturing relationships. The customer experience is just another way for you to set yourself apart from the competition and building lasting and loyal followers.

CHAPTER 6

We're Talking Money

Ahh money. Everyone's favorite subject! We all seem to love money but have the hardest relationship with it. Especially business owners. We tend to work from a place of lack versus a place of abundance. I get it. Cash flow is the life force that keeps you going but it's the lack of activity amongst business owners to manage it, that sink businesses faster than Titanic.

I was a hustler and probably always will be. If there was a job that I could do to make extra money, then I'd volunteer. By 18, I was a hostess, to go server, and my newest position, Admin. This was my first introduction to bookkeeping and combined my love of math and the real world.

Every morning, I looked at the night before's numbers, check out system's sales reports and made sure everything balanced. Comps, discounts, cash, credit cards, tips, and the deposit all had to balance and if it didn't, I had to find out why. Most of the time if it didn't balance the managers on duty the night before new why or there was a technical glitch that couldn't be solved until the morning.

Numbers and math come easily to me but I know it's difficult for many business owners. Or at least that's the story they tell themselves. I bet you tell yourself that too. The managing money side of things can be fun. YES, FUN! You got to make it a game. Numbers tell a story. There are no secrets.

Cash may be king, but DATA IS QUEEN. Just like in chess, the Queen is powerful and protects the king. In business it's the information that the numbers give you that protects your profits and grows your business. Once you learn to love numbers, it all becomes a fun game.

MONEY MANAGEMENT

I've worked both corporate and local places and all of them manage their books on the daily. The key things I took away from years doing the bookkeeping work: close your books every night and review them every morning, always review your sales goals, and review your budget weekly.

CLOSING THE BOOKS/REVIEWING

Now in the accounting world, you don't close your books until year end but here I'm talking about settling the day's transactions so you can start fresh the next day. For high volume transactional businesses like restaurants, retail, ecommerce, etc.

it's imperative to keep up on the daily or you risk losing money from simple fixes.

I once had a restaurant bookkeeping client that was having serious cash flow issues. They were not keeping up with their books daily and never reconciled their bank statements monthly. By the time I received them, we had to do some serious cleanup work and I set them up on a cash flow spreadsheet to monitor the bank accounts, credit card deposits, and expenses.

While cleaning up their books from a previous year, I caught a discrepancy between a written check and what was cashed by the bank. The check was written for $36.00 but they way the check was written the decimal looked like a tiny zero. Even though the check was written in words for thirty-six dollars, the bank cashed it for $360.00. Neither bank caught the mistake and neither did the restaurant owners! We were too far past the date of the transaction so there was nothing we could do to recuperate the loss.

Fast forward, to current day books, I was monitoring the bank accounts and saw two transactions of $50 to an unknown vendor. The managers had no idea who they were, so I called the vendor and did some digging. It turns out that someone took the routing number and account number off the check used to pay them, to pay their credit card bill. They did small amounts hoping no one would catch it, but I did.

As much as we tried to help when we stepped in, they had unfortunately had to close their doors. By the time we stepped in to help, they had already three years of bad money management habits that were too much to overcome.

This story I wish was a rare one but in my bookkeeping career and the restaurants that I work at, it's the ones that don't keep up with their books that make bad decisions and ultimately close. You might be a solopreneur and think, you don't have to do it so often but I've seen and even done it myself, accidentally use the wrong card when purchasing stuff.

You may not have hundreds of transactions a day that warrant daily bookkeeping but keeping a strict schedule on doing your books and reviewing is important. I wouldn't do anything less than weekly. Biweekly and monthly can easily put you behind.

The bookkeeping can help you stay on top of sales goals, catch unnecessary expenses, see what products/services are working, catch sales trends by day, month, and even seasons. Is a merchant vendor taking too long to get your payments processed and deposited? Find a better one. These are the questions you should be asking yourself so you can keep expenses down and sales productivity up.

ALWAYS REVIEW SALES GOALS & BUDGET

Before business hours started, we would review the days sales goals, what we did last year, what we did the week before, were there outstanding factors? (was there a special event in town, students out on break, etc., big promotional blast from the company, etc.). You always wanted to be better or around the same as you were the last year. You should be pushing for growth.

The things I took from this are, always be better than you were before (never settle) and look at where you were and what you can do now. Every shift we would have what was called a pre-shift. A mini shift meeting to talk about what's going on for day, any specials, sales contests, and out of stock items. This the staff informed to make better decisions out in the restaurant to provide better service and boost sales. We would feature a different item each shift, highlight it and teach sales strategy points for that item.

If the company or our store managers saw a dip in sales for a particular item, we would do a push to re-educate the staff to see if we could make sales. If sales dropped on a menu item because the staff isn't talking about it, then we've remedied the issue. If we've done this and sales didn't increase well enough, it might be time to evaluate if the item is worth carrying.

When you're tracking your sales goals, it's not just about the number goal. Look at your offerings, your sales approach, and what outside factors that could harm or help you.

The same goes for your budget. Are you staying on target with your budget? Are you prepared for one-time expenses or annual expenses?

Things you need to be reviewing on your budget:
1. Are you meeting sales goals? What do you need to do to achieve them?

2. Are there any new or unexpected events near you or that affect your industry that could affect sales both positively and negatively?

3. Are you overspending in certain areas? Underspending in certain areas? What factors may be contributing to this? What can you do to mitigate unnecessary spending?

4. Payroll. You may not have employees but work with contractors. See if you're keeping people on the clock longer than you need. Are clock-in and clock-outs correct? Do you have a full-time contractor but have part time work? Look to see how you can re-package services for a lower price so you're only paying for what you need.

5. Check sales forecasts and cash flow balance.

RECORDKEEPING

Organization is key to stay on top of everything! I talk more about streamlining your processes and systems in the next chapter. When it came to bookkeeping, you have to document EVERYTHING! I mean you bought something with cash, we still need the receipt. This is still one of the biggest faux pas I see business owners make. They think just because it's cash that it's not really a big deal but that's a disrespect to your business and your money.

Not keeping receipts and documenting cash purchases leads to you losing out on possible tax deductions or reducing your taxable revenue. Why would you want to lose that? I've worked for global multi-million-dollar corporate restaurants; they would not tolerate anything over or under $3 balancing for each day. Everywhere I've worked, we were always within a dollar.

These corporations didn't grow by disregarding small transactions like cash transactions so why should we as small business owners? When more times than not, small business owners need to be watching their cash flow a lot more than the big guys, especially new businesses.

Recordkeeping doesn't have to be tedious and you can always hire the right talent to help. I do emphasize how important it is as the owner or CEO, even though you are not doing the bookkeeping, you are always in communication with whomever is doing it because at the end of the day you are making the big decisions for your company. You can't do it without keeping track of your financial health. Track what you want to attract.

CASH IS KING

Cash is king. Period. Business that doesn't have more cash flowing in, than going out, go extinct. It is not enough to be lean and cut expenses but you need to grow sales. When I use to admin, we would do daily deposit drops for the restaurant. The faster the cash is in your account the more cash you have available to cover expenses.

For restaurants, the two biggest expenses were payroll and food costs. There's no getting around needing supplies every day and keeping a staff to keep the doors open. So, getting those cash deposits into the bank was critical.

It is no different for any small business, whether it be retail or service oriented. I've had past clients who made it difficult to pay themselves or get their money quicker! They spent too much time running around getting paid. I had one client who didn't want to pay merchant fees so would only accept cash or check. Checks these days, especially large ones, go on hold for days. As for cash not many people carry that much cash anymore, so she wasn't making it any easier for her customers as well.

Another client of mine was having trouble with PayPal keeping her money for a month before releasing it. We researched some alternatives with comparable rates and integrated those. Now she automatically gets deposits in her account within two days without having to do anything.

If you can't get around getting paid faster for a certain product or service make sure you have other payment gateways that can get you paid faster. Like I mentioned in chapter 3, make it easier for people to pay you and quicker for you to receive it. Do you charge a monthly service? Have them sign up for automatic payments for a small percentage off as an incentive.

For better cash flow, cut unnecessary expenses, increase sales, and make it faster to get paid.

CHAPTER 7

Processes & Systems

Staying organized and consistent is important for any business to be successful and grow. We've all worked that job or had a manager where you had to do it the "corporate" way or it wasn't right. It is annoying. There is something to be said about consistency. These companies didn't become multi-million-dollar corporations without putting some processes and systems in place.

DOCUMENT EVERYTHING

STANDARD OPERATING PROCEDURES

Small businesses and even one-person shows (a.k.a. solopreneurs) don't have S.O.P.'s, Standard Operating Procedures. Standard Operating Procedures are step by step guides that establish company standards in all aspects of running the business. If you are a one-person show, you shouldn't need one, right? Wrong. Having your processes written down will keep you consistent and on task. When you are ready to grow your team and onboard new team members, it'll be easier to train them versus scrambling to put things together.

It's going to be tedious at first, but you'll be grateful later. Standard Operating Procedures should be accessible to all team members. This helps institute consistency, efficiency, and set clear expectations. It also keeps you in compliance with the laws and industry regulations.

Restaurants can definitely be under a lot of scrutiny since they're in the realm of public health. Standard Operating Procedures will take into account the local county health regulations, on top of the company's standards. Standard Operating Procedures will affect how you train and set expectations for quality of work.

You may not think there are any laws or regulations in your industry, however there could be legal issues that could affect your work. Do you hire freelance writers for your website? You would create an S.O.P for how to create, review, and edit content. If one of your writer's didn't cite a source or your assistant added a copyrighted photograph without the right permissions, you could be hit with legal trouble.

I don't recommend hiring a staff without standard operating procedures in place, so take the time to put things in order.

TRAINING MATERIALS

For each position in the restaurant, we had a guide for trainers to follow. Training would be 3-4 days and each day the trainer had specific things to go over, so it would not overwhelm the trainee. Each new day of training, we would review and build on the training from the day before.

Nowadays, there are a plethora of resources to create training videos for e-learning. I'm a big fan of on the job training but for remote workers or if you manage several locations for your business, creating training videos can cut time and expenses. A combination on e-learning and hands-on training can solidify skills.

BOOKKEEPING

You should have a system in place for paying bills, reviewing accounts receivables, entering data into your accounting platform, and filing. Having a system in place ensures nothing gets missed or there aren't any questions.

When I used to admin, I had to follow certain steps to get the day started. First, I'd verify tips were calculated and entered correctly in the payroll system. Next, I'd verify the deposit was correct, counted the drawers, and made sure petty cash balanced. Then, I'd proceed by entering invoices into our system. Once I was done, I'd initial and date the invoices, signifying they were entered, and file them.

At the store level we didn't pay the invoices, but as a small business you'll be in charge to make sure bills get paid on time. All of this should be documented in your SOP. Will bills be reviewed every day for payment, once a week, etc.? How often are you following up on invoices needing to be paid by clients? Balancing the books, reconciling accounts, and paying taxes are all things, you will need to sit down and figure out.

HUMAN RESOURCES

This might be my least favorite subject to talk about and most likely everybody's least favorite subject, haha. You may not be at the point of supporting a team. If so, go ahead and skip it BUT I'd definitely tag this section for when you're ready.

I remember the many, many, many orientations I've conducted throughout my career. I created checklists for myself so I could keep track of everything. I scheduled the classes, called the new employees to confirm they could make it, reminded them to bring two forms of identification and their bank account info for direct deposit.

Getting this stage right is the first impression your new employees/contractors are going to see of you. If you're disorganized and flaky, they will come to expect that from you. Remember, people can work anywhere and with anyone, they don't have to just impress you, but you have to impress them as well.

Whether you're hiring contractors, such as virtual assistants, social media managers, or graphic designers, or ready to support a staff, you still need to have the proper systems and paperwork in place.

Employees:

- Personnel files (*job description, offer letter, application, reviews, promotions/raises, disciplinary actions, references, sick time/leave of absence/vacation tracking, signed employee handbook, other company related forms. This folder should not have any forms that have private information on it that could be in violation of HIPAA, The Health Insurance Portability and Accountability Act of 1996*)
- I9's need to be in a separate area (*Ideally in a binder locked away in a cabinet or safe where not everyone has access, only upper management*)
- Private file (*this file should be kept away from the personnel file and locked away. This file will contain any paperwork that may contain medical records such as doctor's notes, medical leave, FMLA request forms, direct deposit forms with bank account info, anything with a social security number.*)

Keeping employee records is a legal requirement. I'd check with your local and federal laws to keep you in compliance. Forms like disciplinary action or reviews, are recommended to keep on file. in the unfortunate case of an unlawful termination suit or other litigation. As painful as paperwork is, it could be key you out of hot water.

Contractors:

- Contractor file (*completed W9, insurance policies [if applicable], contractor agreement, and references, print communication like letters and proposals, copy of 1099's issued*)
- Invoices

I've never worked anywhere where they didn't keep contractor files. You are not legally obligated to keep records on contractors. There are strict guidelines of who are employees and independent contractors. In the event you're accused of misclassifying an individual working for you, your records are there to support. There are steep penalties if you do misidentify someone working for you.

There are several companies going digital for record keeping. Whichever program you choose to store your records, it should be HIPAA compliant and on a secured server. You'll be liable for any data breaches and leaking of personal private information.

There are several hr/payroll companies, bookkeepers, and accountants that can handle this for you. You may still need to do the work of getting the contractors and employees to fill out paperwork. Regardless, if you have someone else doing the work, be sure to be in communication so you understand what is going on. At the end of the day, it is your business on the line.

WORKFLOWS

The flow of a shift was like a dance. I loved starting the business day as the staff started to show up and prepare for the busy moments. In order for the day to go smooth there were workflows in place in every aspect of the restaurant.

The managers were getting the day started by checking numbers, sales trends, yesterday's shift notes, making sure the money banks for the drawers were set, and check on staffing for the night.

Then you had the prep cooks who are the real MVPs. They come in and prep exactly what we need for the day. It's a fine dance between prepping too little and too much. That's where the kitchen managers came in. They went over numbers, inventory, and what needed to be stocked for a successful night.

Then as it's a couple of hours before opening business hours, you'll have your openers come in and set up for the day. The bartenders setting up and prepping for the night. Servers were making the coffee and tea, and setting up the server stations. The hostess laid out menus at tables and stocking silverware. Then you had line cooks setting up their respective stations.

As business doors opened to the public, the rest of the staff came in at staggering times. This helped meet the needs of the restaurant and optimize the usage of labor. The two biggest costs for a restaurant are food and labor. For restaurants to be profitable, they need to optimize both workflows and processes. In an ideal shift, you'd be well staffed at the right times all the time. Anyone who's been in the industry, knows that's not always the case.

Creating workflows not only makes the job or project smoother, it creates consistency. You don't miss anything with workflows because they keep you organized. You'll have a better understanding on how long a task should take. Workflows are great for the day to day repeatable tasks.

Some workflows you should create, and if you can automate them, even better.

- Onboarding new team mates
- Content marketing
- Social media marketing
- Sales pipeline
- Each job position's duties
- Paying bills and filing
- Sending out invoices and getting paid
- Onboarding of clients
- Bookkeeping and review of financial statements
- Customer Service
- Delivery of goods/services

You may have some particular workflows for your business or industry. To maximize productivity, automating your workflows are best. This allows you more time to focus on your strengths and revenue generating activities. There are several project management programs. Some have templates already made but you can also customize for your business.

PLAN, EXECUTE, TRACK, & REVIEW

There will be moments in your business that aren't day to day but will need a system in place to handle. Such things are product/service development, a marketing campaign, special events, or writing this book.

Plan

For special one-off projects or first-time projects, be sure to plan for any possible contingencies, timeline/schedule of tasks, labor, paperwork, and legal (*i.e. licensing, contracts, etc.*). The devil is in the details. It's usually the thing you tell yourself that will never happen...well it happens. Not planning for these things will cost you time and money.

I've worked with three places that had event planners. Now I'm running my own catering company. I know every event is unique but some of the basic tasks are the same. For those, you should have a workflow in place. For events, we needed to get the number of guests for the event, the menu solidified, special details like audio visual needs, and as a caterer, we ask whether the venue has potable water and outlets near our station.

I will ask my clients before we book them questions that help us do the job more efficiently and tailored to their experience.

- What is their theme?
- Is the event casual versus formal
- What is the color scheme, among other things?

These random questions, which may seem random, help me get a feel of what type of event they want. I can craft the food and experience to match what they want.

When planning for your workflows or project, keep top of mind schedules, how long things may take, buffer in time for unexpected situations (if applicable) and then execute.

Execute & Track

I've seen this a million times, you do the research, make the plan, but don't execute. I've been a part of several menu development stages and special company events. We'd get stuck in the brainstorming phase and then things will fizzle and the plan never comes to fruition.

Be decisive. From product development to marketing campaigns, you have to take action. If there are mistakes or mishaps, those are learning experiences. Track what went well and what changes you needed to make and why along the way. The notes will help you fine tune the process for the future or whether you need to scrap the project altogether.

Review

Whenever an event ended, we would review what went well and what didn't. What was in our control and what wasn't. How can we make the process smoother next time and did we learn any new lessons? Don't spend too much time in this stage. You're here as an observer to make things more efficient for you and your team in the future.

CHAPTER 8

Productivity

As the owner, you wear many hats. Juggling all the duties, even with a team, can be overwhelming. I went through similar situations as a server, bartender, and manager. Everything has to get done, so where do you even start? There have been several times as an entrepreneur where the workload got overwhelming and all I wanted to do was take a nap. Seriously. I'll share a story of when I had to manage a very busy dinner rush as a server and how I've applied that same mindset to get things done in my business.

Real Life Anecdote #1:

It's a busy Friday evening for dinner. I got done taking a drink order from my table, I watch the hostess give me two more tables. I still have to take the order from my first table. I want to pull my hair out. Mind you, we have to greet a table within 30 seconds and get drinks to the table within two minutes. What do I do?

I greet the two tables that just sat down. I let them know I'll be getting to them as soon as possible. They're happy and look over the menu. I check on the table that needs to order and tell them I'll be right back to take their order.

In the kitchen, I put in drink orders for table two, grab waters and bread for the new tables. I drop off drinks at table two, waters and bread for the new table, take their drink and appetizer orders. After this, I swing back to table one to take their order.

As I put in all the orders I need, I'll ask another server to drop off bread and water refills to my section. I check the status on current orders, grab any soda refills, and run food out. You have to have full hands in and full hands out.

I swing by table two to take their orders, check on the table three and four and if they're enjoying their appetizer. I walk past table one and eye if they need anything. I try not to bother or ask if I don't need to.

I could keep going but this is how the cycle goes.

What helped me be a great server AND efficient, was I had to learn how to plan ahead, ask for help, and prioritize.

PLAN AHEAD

I knew I had deadlines to meet as a server. The above situation, I experienced every weekend. I had to figure out how to meet company standards, guest's expectations, and make that money. When I say plan ahead, I really mean look ahead in the timeline.

- What still needs to get done?
- What can you actually get done?
- What needs to get done RIGHT NOW?
- What do you need to handle and what can others help you with?
- Who can you ask for help?
- What do I need to say no to?
- What tasks can I piggyback on each other to maximize time?

Ask yourself these questions when planning your day to day, or projects. The three questions I always ask myself first are:

1. What needs to get done RIGHT NOW?
2. What can I actually get done?
3. What do I need to say no to?

If I know what I can do and how much time I have, it's easier to answer the other questions. I drop what I can't do and look for people who can help me in those areas. If I can't do it, then I say no to it. Whether it's taking on another client or for the above story example, I won't take a table. If I can't give my best, then I won't take it on.

WHAT NEEDS TO GET DONE RIGHT NOW?

Look at what needs to get done right now. Such things are client focused work. Do you have sessions or meetings with your clients? Reviewing client work? If you produce products, are you fulfilling purchase orders on time? Following up on client projects or communication? Those things are of immediate importance.

Next, look at revenue generating activities. What are you doing to bring in more customers?

- Social media content
- Meetings with potential clients
- Meetings with partners and vendors
- Sales campaigns
- Prospecting

Are you on track with bringing in enough leads? What do you need to review here and adjust?

WHAT CAN I ACTUALLY GET DONE?

You're going to have to get real with yourself here. Even superheroes have their limitations. What are the things that only you can truly do? Maybe only you can produce the products but can you get help with the packaging the orders and sending them out? Only you can work with the client but can you automate scheduling sessions and follow up emails?

Do you create all the content for your website and social media accounts? Have someone else edit and post them for you. Batch creating content to also save time. Remember when I asked, "What tasks can I piggyback on each other to maximize time?" Start thinking about this when it comes to your do list.

WHAT DO I NEED TO SAY NO TO?

My biggest struggle is the question, "What do I need to say no to?" I'm a born people pleaser. When I believe in something, I like to go all in. I found too many times, I've overextended myself. All to shortchange quality in all my endeavors. Just because you want to do something, doesn't mean you need to do it now. It's important to keep your current goals top of mind when deciding what to say yes to and what to say no to.

Make a list of things you want or need to do with your business. What is the most pressing to bring in money now? Is it creating products/services? Learning marketing strategies? Is it going out and networking? Whatever it is, do one first, master it, and then move on to the next. Check out the Prioritize section in this chapter for more tips.

ASK FOR HELP

This is the most difficult for many entrepreneurs., including myself. There is a sense of loss of control when you ask others. Yet, I've never been successful without other people helping. As a business owner, you need to focus on your strengths and places where you're irreplaceable. Automate some systems and/or hire some people. Make sure your time is best spent on revenue generating activities. You'll want to provide the best experience to your clientele.

This extends to your personal life too. Have kids? Get a nanny or ask friends or family for a couple of hours a day, so you can focus on your business. Your first thought might be, "Tina Marie, I don't have the money to pay for help!" I'm going to ask you something. "How much are you worth hourly in your business?" Is it $50, $100, $500?

How much are you losing by focusing on things that don't matter? Could you afford that nanny, housekeeper, assistant, if you got to focus on the right things? Start looking at things as an investment. You are a whole, creative, and resourceful human being. I bet you can find free or affordable solutions until you can grow into hiring people.

PRIORITIZE

When people ask me how I balance work and life with running two businesses, leading a nonprofit and a personal life. I tell them, I don't. I just prioritize. Sometimes, I have to say no to fun nights out with friends. Sometimes, it means saying no to a business opportunity.

When you are first starting a business, your social life and sleep may suffer greatly. You're in the building stage. I've learned the hard way that all work and no play leaves you burned out, unproductive and unhappy. You should be building your business for sustainability, not just for profit. One day you'll find yourself growing rapidly with no one to help, completely overwhelmed.

How I prioritize everything in my life is simply asking, "Is this a hell yeah?" If I'm not 100% about it, I won't do it. If it's a maybe, then I'll table it to review in the future. In order to manage "time" and balance your work and personal life, you have to know what your bandwidth is, what your goals are, and be flexible.

YOUR BANDWIDTH

We are blessed with a certain amount energy a day. Imagine you're a car and your energy level = the gas tank. A lot of stop and go traffic in the city is going to use up more gas than say taking the freeway. What tasks burn you out quickly or use up more mental energy? If you can't outsource them, what days and times do you work at your peak? Schedule those tasks for that time.

CHAPTER 9

Leadership

This career has taught me how to do so many things right but it also taught me what not to do. Leadership in itself is a tough thing to master. I had many great managers but also not so great managers. I know when I first became a shift manager at 21, I had so much to learn. I thought I knew it all. I was a tough cookie, demanded high standards, and would get upset it they didn't. I was also not in a great place in my personal life and that spilled over into work.

I'll admit that I was a terrible manager back then, burned out and completely unhappy. So much so, that when I left that job, I turned down a salaried manager position at the next place. I just wanted to be a server and finish school. Later in my career, I went on to be an assistant manager at two different companies. I vowed to do a better job this time.

I realized I wasn't meant to be a manager, at least not at a corporate company. There were such strict rigid rules to follow.

The corporate mindset didn't allow management to be creative and resourceful.

If we didn't make sales enough to cover labor costs, we had to cut all hourly staff off the floor. There were several shifts where only the managers were on to run the store. The company only view the data as important versus looking at it from a holistic point of view.

I know I said to be data driven and learn to love numbers. I don't want you to be so involved in it that you lose focus on what's the really important, *your people*. Feed into your team. Foster an environment of creativity and innovation. There are things that set managers and leaders apart. First, we'll take a look at the difference between the two. Then, we'll dive into the three skills every leader should have and finally mentorship.

MANAGER VS LEADERS

It took me awhile to understand the true difference between a manager and a leader. Having a manager mindset isn't bad. Having a blend of both leadership skills and managerial skills will set you apart. Knowing when to exercise either trait, takes emotional intelligence, practice, and time.

The bosses I hated working for had a managerial mindset. Mangers have a "do as I say" view point. They only look at the short term and often only did enough so they wouldn't get into trouble. A managerial mindset views people as replaceable, not assets. They always saw a problem and rarely awarded praise for a job well done. I never felt appreciated with these bosses.

Yes, there are times where things need to be done a certain way or need to get done and right. Yet, if the team have ideas which could streamline their job, why wouldn't want to listen to their feedback?

I once told my boss about a new scheduling app. The company had maybe been five years old at the time. Created by restaurant managers, it was an innovative scheduling app for restaurants. The company, with stores nationwide, surprised me with schedules still made on excel sheets. We had to come into the store to get our schedules. If you wanted a shift picked up, good luck coordinating with managers for approval. You'd also be lucky if it was communicated to the rest of the management staff.

I told my boss about the app because it had great tools for the managers because I had used it as a manager. They had a log book so managers could write shift notes. You could create templates for schedules, shift changes, time off requests, block off busy days so no one could ask for it off. The schedule was always up to date and accessible, allowing managers accurately hold staff accountable for their schedule.

He laughed at me and asked if it costs money. He made it seem like a ridiculous idea and that I shouldn't have brought it up. Just over a year later, the company was under new management and guess what? They implemented the scheduling app and my manager was raving how much he loved the site.

He had such a bottom-line point of view. He didn't see the benefits or the ROI (return on investment) the site could offer him. Streamlined communication and more time for important tasks, for the management staff alone, was a huge benefit. No longer did managers have to track down notes on time requested off, jump on the phone to approve time or wonder who was going to show up for their shift.

My boss at Outback© was very big about cross training positions and training up. As I watched through the years, I saw the value of doing this and it was brilliant. We would offer opportunities to team members that were eager and performed well at their jobs. This gave employees opportunities for more hours and opened up our options for scheduling. There was always a probationary period with the new position. We would evaluate how well they did. If they did well, they'd be the first to move into that position full time and they would train their replacement.

If you were a top bartender and trainer, you'd be offered a position as shift manager. When I was shift manager, my boss taught me inventory management and liquor ordering. I also was taught scheduling and closing the restaurant. These were all things an assistant manager would do and I wasn't required to do them at all. As I learned these things, he was teaching the assistant managers some aspects of his job.

This allowed for each position a better understanding of the restaurant and what the position above us had to handle. By doing this, my boss set us up for success when we are ready to move up. He knows he has skilled talent that can do the job already, when a position opens up. He was never worried about someone replacing him. He had the forethought to cultivate a management team that could handle running the store when he's not there.

| *"It's a marathon, not a race." – Original Origin Unknown*

Most small business owners aren't able to grow because they are stuck with a short-term gains mindset and unable to give up control. Every decision you make should not be made with the thought of "What will I lose?", but from the mindset of "How will this help me grow?" Leaders look for opportunities, managers look for problems.

Don't have a staff yet? No worries. Employing the same mindset when you show up for your clientele, audience, and yourself is just as important. My old boss use to say, "*It's a marathon, not a race.*" So many new entrepreneurs are trapped with shiny object syndrome and the fear of missing out. They never stick long enough with something to learn it and implement it. Even worse, they try it, don't see immediate results and give up.

The marketing traps of "*6 Figures in 6 Months*" or "*I became a millionaire in 2 years*" definitely get people interested and buying. What these guys aren't telling are the years of struggle, trial and error before things seem to have "clicked". What they're teaching you is what finally worked for them.

Leaders are willing to take risks, fail, and find what works best for them. This is what we call in the industry, "best practices." Managers are afraid to take risks because they only see what they could lose, not what they could gain. Every mistake, every fail is an opportunity for growth.

> *BONUS LEADERSHIP TIP:*
> *When I first trained to become a server, we had four days of training and we had a different trainer for each day. The idea behind this was to see how all the best servers did the job. Everyone has their unique strengths. Maybe one trainer was a great salesman, another was great at meeting silent service, another was great at managing several tables and not drop the ball. The goal at the end of training was to not only learn the job but take the best practices of each trainer and incorporate into your own style.*
>
> *When learning anything in your business, find the top experts in that field. Figure out what they each do best in their own way. Find a way to take what they each do best and make it work in a way that feels authentic and right for you.*

THE 3 D'S

Would you rather have more time enjoying life or always working in your business? How would it feel knowing you could work less and make more money? I believe most us pick a business that could run smoothly without us always there.

Yet many us (including this recovering Type A Perfectionist) have a tough time releasing control. If we are continuously working in our business versus on it, we will never see growth. I've seen so many of my colleagues and clients too afraid to relinquish control. I get it. Your business is your baby. You've put so much thought, sweat equity, and time to grow it. You have a vision; can you trust anyone to help you execute it?

"I want to do less one to one client work but I don't know if I can trust someone else to give the care and attention that I do."

"I want to hire someone but I don't want to put the time and effort into them and they don't stay. I need someone to be here a while."

"They keep making mistakes. It's just easier for me to do it then correct them."

Any of this sound familiar? The truth is things will never work out the way you want it the first time. Each opportunity is a way for you to learn more of what you do want and are looking for. To better prepare for growth, master delegating, development, and damage control.

DELEGATING

Delegating tasks that take up too much of your time, frees you up to do more important things. Remember in chapter 8, when I talked about prioritizing your tasks and asking for help? This is what I'm talking about. Focus on your strengths, revenue generating activities, and the most important/pressing matters.

Entrepreneurs and business owners who try to do, burn out quickly. If you are starting out and bootstrapping, hiring help may not be an option. There are resourceful ways to get things done that are free or low cost. Try swapping services with another professional who might need your services too. Look for software that can automate some tasks. Check out freelancers on places like UpWork or Fiverr. Ask friends or family to help with personal errands. Just ask.

DEVELOP

The key to feeling more confident and trusting others is watching them grow. There is no way around growing your business and vision without the help of others. People management will always play a large factor in your success. I don't know a single restaurant/bar that succeeded without the people behind it.

Can you imagine walking into a restaurant where the server took your order, had to answer the phones, made the food, made the drinks, and took payment? Would you have a great experience? I don't think so. Why would you run your business like this?

Take the time and effort to invest in people. There is not one successful six to seven figure company that is ran by one person alone. You may not find the right people at first, but each opportunity brings clarity on what you're really looking for. I talk more about building a team in chapter 10.

DAMAGE CONTROL

Things will go wrong and oftentimes at the worst time. A smooth shift at the restaurant was a rare beauty to behold. Most times, we're putting out fires and trying to prevent them. From running out of key ingredients, missing deliveries, staff calling out, and more, you had to learn resourcefulness and resiliency very quickly.

If the prep cook over prepped a certain dessert, we'd make it a sales contest that night to minimize waste. If the someone called out, we'd jump on the phone and call down the staff list to see if someone could fill in. Oh, a 15-person party just walked in with no reservation at prime dinner time? Let's find a place with the shortest wait for them.

You see, the industry taught me there was not one problem that didn't have a solution. We didn't shut the restaurant down that night because three people called out sick. If there was no way to fix it, for example, the distributor is on back order for a liquor in our signature drink. We'd say it's unavailable and suggest something else.

Your business will go through trials, some small, some big. Start thinking of what you can do to minimize the "damage", find alternatives, and execute. Success is about picking yourself up and looking at all the possibilities.

MENTORSHIP

Mentorship has helped me grow both professionally and personally. I had mentors in almost every position I had. My knowledge and skills are attributed to those who took the time to teach me but most importantly the why. I'm a person that needs to understand why a certain method or strategy works. So, I apply this in my own teaching and coaching strategies.

Mentorship goes both ways. I've found as I grew professionally, helping others not only honed my skills but also helped me gain invaluable interpersonal skills. I had a sense ownership in what I did and loved seeing people flourish with my guidance.

HAVING A MENTOR

I would not be a great bartender if it wasn't for the many great bartenders that trained me. The coaching didn't stop after official training days either. When you have a mentor, you don't just get their career length experience and knowledge. You get all the people who taught them as well. They've taught me how to do things and what not to do (sometimes those are the best lessons). When they learned something new, they didn't hesitate to share with me as well.

I don't think I would have survived the management life if it weren't for my mentors. Being a restaurant manager is *tough*. I'm not saying that being a manager at an office or anywhere else isn't tough. For management in restaurants, there are long hours and sometimes without breaks. You're dealing with fiery and stressed out people (guests and staff). You're always putting out fires because there isn't a shift where everything is smooth. I've learned a lot on how to reduce or prevent fires, motivating staff, and coaching techniques to boost productivity.

When looking for a mentor, find someone who is great in their field AND you have a great rapport with. Mentor and mentee relationships can be long lasting. I still reach out to my old mentors for advice! Sometimes a mentor will seek you out and don't waste the opportunity. You may not always agree with your mentor but be open and understanding on what they share with you.

BEING A MENTOR

It's tough finding time to build your empire, juggle family, personal life, and professional development. But there is a sense of satisfaction in giving back and sharing your knowledge with a mentee. For me, I've been able to revisit basic skills that I've let slide. We often think we know something or dismiss it because it's simple. Sometimes getting back to basics helps you hone your skills even further.

One time, I had been bartending for years and became complacent. One of the servers wanted to become a bartender. We weren't moving anyone up anytime soon. So, I recommended she learn as much as she can about the alcohol and improve her liquor sales. We took the time to focus on one category first. I'd teach about vodka and quiz her and so on. Not only did she improve, but I did!

There was something about teaching someone else which helped reaffirm what I already knew. This not only pull me out of my rut but made me a better salesperson as well. I've found by coaching others in business that it's made me look at my own practices. Have I been letting certain areas slip? Where can I get back on track?

Mentorship is completely different than coaching and consultation. Coaching helps the individual find their own strengths and guides them in finding their own answers that are right for them. Consultants give advice on how to strengthen the business. Mentors are more invested in growing the individual. They aid in growing their strengths, their skills, and overall success.

CHAPTER 10

Building a Team

Building a solid team for your business may be the hardest thing to do. I've hired and fired many people in my career. Neither is easy to do. Hiring people requires a lot of trust and letting go of some control. This in itself is difficult for many business owners. At some point, in order to grow, you'll have to build a team.

I didn't realize there were so few resources out there about developing a team until I started getting a lot of questions about what to do. There are plenty of resources on the technical side of hiring but not many resources on finding the right people. What do you do when you need to fire someone?

I have learned a few things that I'll share with you. First, it is incredibly important to understand your company culture. Cultivating a team takes time with some trial and error. The biggest thing you'll need in your tool box is clear communication.

COMPANY CULTURE

I talked a little bit about company culture in chapter one. This is key in understanding your leadership style and how people will work together. You'll want people who will understand your vision, support your mission, and are great team players.

Things you should take note before hiring:
- How do you want to lead?
- What type of people are you looking for?
- What kind of environment do you want to provide for your teammates for optimal productivity and creativity?
- How is training done?
- Will you have remote workers? Onsite? Combination of both?
- How are you going to communicate with your team and how often?
- What are the types of people that are going to take your vision and run with it? Take it to levels you never dreamed?

Cautionary tale, be weary of hiring friends and family so you can save some money. They may want to support you but they may not have the skills or traits that are a right fit. I'm not saying you can't hire friends or family but be selective. Some people may work out! Treat them as you would any other applicant. Set expectations and boundaries to protect your personal relationship.

THE PROCESS

FINDING THE RIGHT PEOPLE

Sometimes honing in on the right people can take some trial and error. You may not know exactly what you're looking for until you work with people that just don't work out. Sometimes people start off great and fizzle out. I call this the honeymoon stage. They're happy to start a new job, eager to look good, but after a while become disenchanted with the work. This is because they're doing work they don't really want to or don't feel challenged.

You can weed out a lot of the people that won't fit in the position or the company. When you are looking at applications and resumes, take a look at their work history. Have they worked several jobs within a relatively short period of time? This is a huge red flag for me. This behavior shows restlessness and they may get bored quickly. Not something you'd want if you're looking for longevity.

How relevant is their work experience to the position they're seeking at your company? If they don't have any, why are they interested in the position? Could they be looking for a career change? I'd caution on saying no to an interview with these candidates. I've seen some talented and hardworking people who've never worked in the industry before.

We usually start them at low level position so they get a feel of how the restaurant works and see if they'd even like it. We'd train them into higher positions if things work out. Look deeper at what they've done and the skills they've acquire along the way. Will they translate to what you're looking for?

When I first learned how to interview, I'd sit in while my boss interviewed people. He taught me one thing that still stands out in my mind. He'd ask questions that weren't specific to the company or the position. He'd ask them what they like to do outside of work. From this, he can ask follow up questions that help him get a picture of the type of person they might be.

For example, we got a lot of college students applying. One interviewee might answer, "I play on a basketball league once a week." My boss who loves sports may talk to the interviewee about the latest going on in professional or college basketball. This builds a rapport and loosens up nerves. Then he'd follow up with a question, "What do you love about the basketball league?" People love to share things that they are passionate about. You can really get an understanding of what makes people tick and what is important to them.

The interviewee might answer, "I love that I get to be active. It's a great way to escape and play with new friends." To my boss, he can glean that the interview could handle the strenuous activity on busy nights and that he may be a great team player. My boss would probably ask more follow up questions to refine the picture he has in his head. If he got the answers he was looking for, then he'd proceed with different questions.

This is a small snippet of what to ask in an interview. Craft your interview questions that get you answers to the type of skills and traits you're looking for. Don't be afraid to ask questions that might seem negative. Since we were very customer service oriented, a question often asked was, "Name a time you had a difficult customer. How did you handle it?" When I'm looking for how well they might work with others, I'd ask, "Have you ever had an issue with a coworker? How did you handle it? What did you learn from the experience?"

For you, you could share a real-life situation that happened in your company and ask them how they'd handle it. Don't be afraid to ask a ton of questions. Just make sure they're pertinent to helping you hire. I'd also get a human resources professional or legal counsel to look over your interview questions before you start. This ensures you are not violating any laws or privacy.

ONBOARDING AND THEN WORK BEGINS

Make sure your onboarding process is as streamlined and welcoming as you would for your clientele. Be clear on how training is going to work, timelines, and what paperwork needs to be turned in. The information might be overwhelming but telling them how they can access the information, provide them copies, and how they can reach you for questions.

Find out how your new teammate learns best and adopt your training technique to that. People are either visual, kinesthetic (hands on), or auditory learners. Provide the training in all these different ways so they can learn quickly! It'll save you both in the long run.

You'll spend a lot of hands on time in the beginning. Some people are superstars and will pick up quickly, some may need more time. Big tip here and a sure sign of true leadership, allow them a safe space to fail. Lessons are learned in mistakes. It's like when you tell a kid not to touch the hot stove and they do it any way. Well, they won't do that again because the mistake will be seared in their minds.

IT DIDN'T WORK OUT, NOW WHAT?

Don't get down on yourself if you got a bad apple or hired the wrong person. Some people interview really well or look great on paper. You end up learning a lot more when you are working with them. Every business has experienced it.

Before you're ready to go to the chopping block, make sure to ask them what they are struggling with and how you can support. Coach them through your expectations, what they missed, and action steps to correct it. If you've done this, recorded disciplinary action, and still see no change... Well, it's time.

Now, I highly recommend talking to a human resources professional or legal counsel on best practices for letting people go in your state. Before you hire and fire, you need to understand your rights as an employer and the employee's rights. How quickly do they need to receive their last paycheck? Some states require the last paycheck to be issued within two days, some a week, or the next pay period. Make sure you stay in compliance!

With that being said, here are a few tips I've learned throughout my career:

- Never fire over text message, email, or phone. (I've never worked at a place that does this but, I've heard horror stories) If you have remote workers, video conferencing is best.
- Have a second person there to witness the interaction. This keeps you accountable in saying and doing the right things. It also protects you from the "he said, she said" deal, if the employee wants to fight back.
- Do it with compassion! These are people by the way! It's always hard to lose a job and they'll have a million things on their mind.
- Be clear on why they're being let go, what happens next, and when they can expect their last paycheck

CLEAR COMMUNICATION

The best managers and companies I worked for had clear communication. By clear communication, I mean full transparency. They shared the sales goals and when expenses were high. They'd share new items and ideas for the next season early. They'd ask the staff for feedback on anything and everything. There was always communication on company wide changes and what we were doing for social impact or outreach.

We would recognize team members both company wide and at our local store.

GOALS

Always communicate with your team, the company goals and where you want to go. This boosts motivation and the team gets creative on supporting you. I've seen a lot of companies and manager talk about goals but don't explain the why. You have to give people a reason to care. It can be as simple as, "We strive at this company to do at least 5% better than the last time." We may say, *"Last year on this date we did, $5,000 in sales. This year we are shooting for $5,250."*

Also breaking goals down to bite-size action steps, makes it easier for team members make progress. We'd paint the picture to the staff that they each would need to sell 3 more desserts or appetizers they normally do. Or suggest selling one more drink at the table or cross sell add-ons. This seems like a likely goal they can strive for.

For you it might mean wanting 10,000 more email subscribers because you know your closing rate is at 20%. At 10,000 more subscribers you can reach your sales goal for the month. You can rally your marketing team and admin team to help. Your marketing team may come up with fantastic ideas for campaigns and social media content. Your admin team can ramp up customer service processes and create a FAQ to minimize emails about the services you provide.

CONSISTENCY

Make sure you are consistent with communicating with your team. Don't like meetings much? Do a weekly email round up on what's going on and invite them to ask questions in a chat for the team. Slack is a great application for this but there are several others out there that work as well. You can then schedule meetings every other week.

Fair warning though, if you are running a bigger company, I don't recommend meeting less than weekly. So much can change quickly in a short period of time. Your team should know exactly when they'll be hearing from you, when you're all meeting, and what topics will be covered.

Meetings and updates aren't the only communication that needs to be consistent. How you train, coach, and discipline your team mates need to be the same every time. There is no confusion on whether someone got preferential treatment or not.

OWNERSHIP OR SELF RESPONSIBILITY

I have so much respect for the companies and managers that owned up to making mistakes. Whether it be a bad product or handling a situation wrong, it made the staff feel there was integrity. We can't expect our team members to take responsibility for mistakes if we don't. The staff is only as strong as it's leader. How they are operating is a direct reflection of the leadership team.

When sharing your mistakes, include what lesson you learned from it. Your team may embody that lesson too and help make sure it doesn't happen again.

Having clear communication at your company allows your team to take ownership and pride in what they do. They feel they are involved in the success of the organization. An engaged and happy team breeds creativity and success! Who doesn't want that?

These aren't the end all be all tips to building a stellar team. But they've definitely attributed to the success and happiness of the staff members and leadership team. I challenge you to look at your own processes and see where you can improve communication.

Yaayy!! You did it!

Thank you so much for reading #RestaurantLife! I hope you've gain valuable knowledge on setting up your business for success! I've seen so much in my 17 years and there is still so much to learn! I only wanted to share the important items to get you started.

I have no doubt you'll be a success too! I hope this inspires you to look at your career with a different lens. How have those experiences taught you to be great? You are not limited to what you have done in the past. They only strengthen who you were meant to be.

Just for finishing this book, I have a special gift for you! Grab your copy of my guide, "Best Apps for Business" today. You can get it here: http://bit.ly/bestappsguide

Much Love & Gratitude,

Tina Marie

P.S. If you have questions, want to say hi, or drop a note on how much you loved the book, email me at tinamarie@profitproject.co. I answer every email myself! 🖤

MEET THE AUTHOR

Tina Marie is a Mindset and Success Coach for multi-passionate entrepreneurs and the founder of the Profit Project. She's worked in the restaurant and bar industry for 17 plus years and currently owns a catering company with her husband. She has worked corporate, such as opening locations for Panera Bread©, and mom and pop restaurants.

She helps her clients empower themselves and take action with clarity and focus by creating a safe space. Her goal is to provide her clients the tools, confidence, and skills to elevate themselves and their business. When she's not helping clients, you can find her reading books on business and mindset or whipping up something delicious in the kitchen.